OOR WULLIE®

THE
BIG
BUCKET OF LAUGHS
JOKE BOOK

BLACK & WHITE PUBLISHING

First published 2015
by Black & White Publishing Ltd
29 Ocean Drive, Edinburgh EH6 6JL

1 3 5 7 9 10 8 6 4 2   15 16 17 18

ISBN: 978 1 91023 000 8

A CIP catalogue record for this book is available from the British Library.

Typeset by Black & White Publishing, Edinburgh
Printed and bound by Nørhaven, Denmark

Contents

Hullo!

Welcome tae my Big Bucket o' Laughs
Joke Book. They say laughter is the best
medicine, so how come Mr Wells the chemist in
Auchenshoogle High Street isnae sellin' my book
in his shop?

I've gathered hunners o' jokes and riddles frae
a' my pals – Fat Bob, Soapy Soutar and Wee
Eck – so if ye've heard ony o' them afore, blame
them. PC Murdoch even offered me a few o' his
gags – they'll be the anes ye dinnae laugh at!

There are mair jokes in this book than I've had
hot dinners and Ma has gi'en me plenty o' them
in my time. Talkin' o' dinners, I think I smell mince
and tatties wi' mealy pudden on the side.
MMM! Gotta go!

Keep smilin'!

Wullie

1

Classroom Capers

Oor Wullie may be wee, but he's nae fool,
He answers aw the questions at his school.

William, you missed school yesterday, didn't you?
Oor Wullie: **No' one bit, miss!**

You don't like coming to school, do you William?
Oor Wullie: **It's not the coming to school part I mind - or the going home... it's the bit in-between I dinnae like!**

Robert, do you sometimes have a cake after a school meal?
Fat Bob: **Aye, stomach-cake!**

William, give me a sentence with 'politics' in it.
Oor Wullie: **Oor parrot Polly ate a clock, an' noo, pollyticks!**

Alexander, why are you doing your multiplicationon the floor?
Wee Eck: **You told me no' tae use tables, miss!**

Soutar, what letters are not in the alphabet?
Soapy Soutar: **The ones in the postbox, miss!**

William, what do Robert the Bruce and Alfred the Great have in common?
Oor Wullie: **They both have the same middle name, miss!**

Soutar, if I had seven apples in one hand and six in my other hand, what would I have?
Soapy Soutar: **Big hands, miss!**

William, I hope I didn't see you looking at Soapy Soutar's exam paper.
Oor Wullie: **Michty me. Ah hope you didnae either, miss!**

Teacher: What is the difference between unlawful and illegal?
Oor Wullie: **Unlawful is doing something wrong. Illegal is a sick bird found in the north o' Scotland, miss!**

William, how are you possibly expecting to get straight A's in the exam?
Oor Wullie: **Ah'll use a ruler, miss!**

William, why are you late for school?
Oor Wullie: **Well, ah wis just obeying the sign, 'School ahead, go slow'!**

William, what's the difference between ignorance and apathy?
Oor Wullie: **Ah don't know an' ah don't care!**

William, if you add 12,397 to 18,149 and then take away 24,628, what would you get?
Oor Wullie: **The wrong answer, miss!**

William, where's the best place to locate the school sick room?
Oor Wullie: **Next to the dinner hall, miss!**

William, how does an Eskimo build his house?
Oor Wullie: **Igloos it th'gither, miss!**

Alexander, what is climate?
Wee Eck: **IF you want to get tae the top o' a hill, you have to climate, miss!**

William, give me a sentence with the word 'think' in it.
Oor Wullie: **IF ah wis swimmin' off Auchenshoogle beach, an' ah couldna swim, ah'd think, miss!**

William, what do you call people who live in Paris?
Oor Wullie: **Parasites, miss!**

William, you have got to be careful.
Words can be very hurtful.
Oor Wullie: **You are right, miss. Ah once dropped a dictionary on ma toes!**

William, name me all the Poles?
Oor Wullie: **North, South an' Tad, miss.**

II

Robert, why is history like a fruit cake?
Fat Bob: **Because it's full o' dates, miss!**

Alexander, what is the difference between a school pupil in Scotland and a school pupil in France?
Wee Eck: **Hunners an' hunners o' miles, miss!**

William, how do you spell 'chrysanthemum'?
Oor Wullie: **Well, miss, if you dinnae ken, how am ah supposed to?**

Soutar, Scots have produced many inventions. Who invented spaghetti?
Soapy Soutar: **MacAronni, miss!**

William, did your Ma and Pa help you with your maths homework?
Oor Wullie: **Naw, miss, ah got them all wrong by myself!**

Primrose, can you tell me where Hadrian's Wall is?
Primrose Paterson: **Roond his garden, miss!**

William, why did early man draw pictures of rhinoceroses and hippopotamuses on their cave walls?

Oor Wullie: **Because they couldnae spell the names, miss!**

William, if you could select anyone in the world to help with your exams, who would it be?

Oor Wullie: **Google, miss!**

William, that was an excellent essay you wrote for someone of your age.

Oor Wullie: **How about for someone of my Ma's age, miss?**

Alexander, name two birds that cannot fly.

Wee Eck: **Twa dead seagulls, miss!**

William, how many seconds are there in a year?

Oor Wullie: **Twelve, miss. The second o' January, the second o' February, the second o' . . .**

William, did you write 'teacher is a bore' on the board?
Oor Wullie: **Sorry, miss. Ah didnae realise you wanted to keep it a secret!**

William, what is the purpose of schools?
Oor Wullie: **Well, miss, without them there'd be nae school holidays!**

Soutar, where is the English Channel?
Soapy Soutar: **Sorry, miss, we dinnae get that on our telly!**

William, how is it that you get so many things wrong in a day?
Oor Wullie: **Ah start early, miss!**

William, I asked you to draw a cow and grass while I was out of the classroom. You've only drawn a cow.
Oor Wullie: **Well, you see, miss, you were out so long the coo ate aw the grass!**

Primrose, is there a word in our language that contains all of the five vowels?
Primrose Paterson: **Unquestionably, miss!**

William, give me the plural of child.
Oor Wullie: **Twins, miss!**

Robert, how many months have 28 days in them?
Fat Bob: **All o' them, miss!**

William, why are you scratching yourself?
Oor Wullie: **Because ah'm the only ane who knows where the itch is, miss!**

William, what does minimum mean?
Oor Wullie: **A wee mummy, miss!**

William, what happened after the wheel was invented?
Oor Wullie: **There was a revolution, miss!**

William, if there are ten flies on a window
and I swat one, how many will be left?
Oor Wullie: **Just the dead one, miss!**

Robert, what is the difference between here and there?
Fat Bob: **The letter 'T', miss!**

William, this letter from your Pa
looks like it was written by you.
Oor Wullie: **That's because he borrowed**
ma pen to write it, miss!

Alexander, what can you tell me about the Dead Sea?
Wee Eck: **Sorry, miss, I didnae**
even know it was sick!

William, you aren't paying attention to me.
Are you having difficulty hearing?
Oor Wullie: **No, miss, ah'm havin'**
trouble listening!

Primrose, today we are doing history.
Tell me who followed Mary the First?
Primrose Paterson: **Her little lamb, miss!**

William, why did Robin Hood steal from the rich?
Oor Wullie: **Because the poor didnae hae any money, miss!**

Soutar, what is the shortest month of the year?
Soapy Soutar: **May, miss. It only has three letters.**

William, when I ask you, I want you to answer at once.
Now, how much is eleven and five?
Oor Wullie: **At once, miss!**

William, why is your report card all wet?
Oor Wullie: **Well, miss, it's because all ma results are below C level!**

*William, I just wish you would
pay me a little attention.*
Oor Wullie: **But, miss, ah'm
paying as little as ah can!**

Alexander, who succeeded the first Scottish king?
Wee Eck: **The second one, miss!**

William, what is the centre of gravity?
Oor Wullie: **'V', miss!**

William, do you know what a duchess is?
Oor Wullie: **The same as an English ess, miss!**

Robert, why do Eskimos eat whale meat and blubber?
Fat Bob: **Crivvens, if ah had tae eat whale
meat ah'd blubber, tae, miss!**

William, please name the four seasons.
Oor Wullie: **Mustard, pepper, salt
an' vinegar, miss!**

*William, what do you think happens to a car
when it gets old and rusty?*
Oor Wullie: **Ma and Pa buy it!**

William, in this country did we ever hunt bear?
Oor Wullie: **Probably no' in the winter, miss!**

Robert, what came after the stone and iron ages?
Fat Bob: **The saus-age, miss!**

*William, I thought I told you to stand
at the back of the queue.*
Oor Wullie: **Ah tried tae, miss, but there
wis somebody there already!**

*William, please put some water in
the classroom fish tank.*
Oor Wullie: **But miss, they
havnae drunk all
the water ah put in
yesterday!**

*William, give me a sentence with
the word 'indisposition' in it.*
Oor Wullie: **Ah always play goalie at the fitba
cause ah like playing in-disposition, miss!**

Robert, what is the coldest country in the world?
Fat Bob: **Chile, miss!**

William, what is the longest night of the year?
Oor Wullie: **A fortnight, miss!**

*Soutar, if two is company and three is a
crowd, what are four and five?*
Soapy Soutar: **Nine, miss!**

William, who was the fastest runner in history?
Oor Wullie: **Adam, miss. He came first
in the human race!**

William, what do you know about oil wells?
Oor Wullie: **Not much, they sound
boring tae me!**

William, didn't you hear me calling you?
Oor Wullie: **But miss, you said no' tae answer you back!**

Alexander, what is a volcano?
Wee Eck: **A mountain wi' hiccups!**

William, should you fight fire with fire?
Oor Wullie: **No, miss. The Fire Brigade uses water!**

Primrose, what's the difference between a buffalo and a bison?
Primrose Paterson: **You cannae wash yer hands in a buffalo, miss!**

William, why can't you ever answer any of my questions?
Oor Wullie: **Miss, if ah could there widnae be any point tae me being in the school!**

William, give me three collective nouns.
Oor Wullie: **A wheely-bin, flypaper an' a vacuum cleaner, miss!**

Soutar, why am I happier when I close my eyes?
Soapy Soutar: **Cause you have nae pupils to see, miss!**

William, why do many birds in Scotland fly south for the winter?
Oor Wullie: **Well, it's easier than walking, miss!**

Alexander, what is the longest word in the dictionary?
Wee Eck: **It's 'smiles', miss. There's a mile between each 's'!**

William, what happened when electricity was invented?
Oor Wullie: **Jings! Somebody got a nasty shock, miss!**

Robert, why did you eat your homework?
Fat Bob: **You said it wis a piece o' cake, miss!**

William, give me a poem about school.
Oor Wullie: **Ah used tae be thin, but noo ah'm thinner. So would you be too wi' oor school dinner!**

Robert, if you are going to yawn in class please put your hand to your mouth.
Fat Bob: **Whit, an' get bitten, miss!**

William, what do you call someone who keeps talking when people are no longer interested?
Oor Wullie: **A teacher, miss!**

Alexander, where did the Vikings land when they came to Scotland?
Wee Eck: **Oan their feet, miss!**

William, name five animals that live in a zoo.
Oor Wullie: **A tiger an' four elephants, miss!**

*Primrose, if you are painting, what colour would
you paint the sun and the wind?*
Primrose Paterson: **The sun rose an'
the wind blue, miss!**

William, what would happen to a plant in our classroom?
Oor Wullie: **If we were doin' maths it might
grow square roots, miss!**

Alexander, why did the Romans build straight roads?
Wee Eck: **It wis so the Scots couldnae lie in
ambush roon the corners, miss!**

William, why are you so poor at decimals?
Oor Wullie: **It's because ah never
see the point, miss!**

*William, are you wearing a sock that is green
and a sock that is blue?*
Oor Wullie: **Aye, an' ah've anither
pair the same at hame, miss!**

William, why shouldn't you write with a broken pencil?
Oor Wullie: **Because it's pointless, miss!**

William, do you like shopping?
Oor Wullie: **No, miss. Once you've seen one shopping centre you've seen a mall!**

William, you weren't at school yesterday.
I heard you were playing football.
Oor Wullie: **That's no' true, an' ah hae the cinema tickets tae prove it, miss!**

Soutar, would you please tell the class why a hummingbird hums?
Soapy Soutar: **Because it doesnae know the words, miss!**

William, you've got your boots on the wrong feet.
Oor Wullie: **But miss, they're the only feet ah've got!**

William, if someone is born in France, grows up in Germany, then comes to Scotland and dies, what are they?
Oor Wullie: **Deid, miss!**

Alexander, what's the opposite of imagination?
Wee Eck: **Ah have nae idea, miss!**

William, what small rivers flow into the River Nile?
Oor Wullie: **The juve-niles, miss!**

William, why did Henry VIII have so many wives?
Oor Wullie: **He liked tae chop an' change, miss!**

Robert, what word is always pronounced incorrectly?
Fat Bob: **Incorrectly, miss!**

Soutar, tell me something about Einstein's Theory of Relativity.
Soapy Soutar: **Well, miss. He had a Ma and Pa, Granny and Granpa...**

William, name twelve animals starting with the letter 'P'.
Oor Wullie: **Six pandas and six panthers, miss!**

*William, how did you get such a good
mark in your English test?*
Oor Wullie: **Ah sat next tae the cleverest
pupil in the class, miss!**

William, you are misbehaving. Go and stand outside.
Oor Wullie: **Help ma boab! Does that mean
ah'm outstanding, miss?**

*Robert, give me a sentence with the word
'fascinate' in it.*
Fat Bob: **Ma overcoat has ten buttons
but ah can only fasten eight, miss!**

*William, why are you so
poor at geography?*
Oor Wullie: **Well, you keep
talking about places ah've
never been tae, miss.**

2

OoR WULLie
and His
Pet Moose, Jeemie

Jeemie is a rare wee moose,
And loves tae stay in Wullie's hoose.

Why does Jeemie need oiling?
Oor Wullie: **Because he squeaks!**

What kind of musical instrument does Jeemie play?
Oor Wullie: **A moose organ!**

What is Jeemie's favourite game?
Oor Wullie: **Hide an' squeak!**

Is it good luck if a cat crosses your path?
Oor Wullie: **No' if yer Jeemie!**

What is grey, hairy and lives on PC Murdoch's face?
Oor Wullie: **His moose-tache!**

What does Jeemie like in his drink?
Oor Wullie: **Mice cubes!**

What did you say to Jeemie when he broke his front teeth?
Oor Wullie: **Hard cheese!**

What is Jeemie's favourite food?
Oor Wullie: **Bubble an' squeak!**

What goes dot, dot, dash, squeak?
Oor Wullie: **Moose code!**

Does Jeemie keep his cage nice and tidy?
Oor Wullie: **Aye, he's always doin' his mousework!**

Does Jeemie carry a brolly?
Oor Wullie: **Aye, tae save him gettin' drookit when it's rainin' cats an' dogs!**

What is small, furry and brilliant at sword fights?
Oor Wullie: **A Mooseketeer!**

What's the difference beween Jeemie and an elephant?
Oor Wullie: **Ma Jeemie maks smaller holes in the skirting board!**

3

OoR WuLLie
and His
Pet Puddock

Wullie's puddock doesn't run or jog,
He only hops . . . for he is a frog.

What happens if your puddock's car is illegally parked?
Oor Wullie: **It gets toad away!**

What jumps up and down in front of cars when it's misty?
Oor Wullie: **Froglights!**

What does your puddock do with paper?
Oor Wullie: **Rip-it!**

If your puddock had a broken leg how would he feel?
Oor Wullie: **Un-hoppy!**

Where does your puddock hang his coat?
Oor Wullie: **In the croak-room!**

What do you call a girl with a puddock on her head?
Oor Wullie: **Lily!**

Can your puddock swim in the sea at Auchenshoogle beach?
Oor Wullie: **Jist knee-deep, knee-deep!**

Why is your puddock always happy?
Oor Wullie: **Because he eats whatever bugs him!**

What kind of shoes does your puddock wear?
Oor Wullie: **Open-toad sandals!**

When is your puddock's favourite time?
Oor Wullie: **During leap years!**

What's your puddock's favourite game?
Oor Wullie: **Croaket!**

Has your puddock ever been in hospital?
Oor Wullie: **Aye, once he had a hopperation!**

What does your puddock drink?
Oor Wullie: **Diet croak!**

4

OoR WULLie
and His
Pet Dog, Harry

Wullie's dog's a nice wee terrier,
Always cheery, nae dog merrier.

Is Harry always in a hurry?
Oor Wullie: No, he's no' a dash-hound!

Wullie, why are you sitting on Harry?
Oor Wullie: Because the teacher told me tae write an essay on ma favourite animal!

What happened when Harry competed against a cat in the milk-drinking contest?
Oor Wullie: Harry lost by three laps!

What's the difference between Harry and fleas?
Oor Wullie: Harry can carry fleas but fleas cannae carry Harry!

What do you give Harry if he has a fever?
Oor Wullie: Mustard. It's the best thing fur a hot dog!

What would Harry do if he swallowed a firefly?
Oor Wullie: He'd bark wi' de-light!

What do you get if you cross a sheepdog with a daffodil?
Oor Wullie: **A collie-flower!**

*What sometimes wears a coat in winter
and pants in summer?*
Oor Wullie: **Harry!**

*How do you stop Harry barking in
the back seat of Pa's car?*
Oor Wullie: **Ah pit him in the front seat!**

Can Harry tell the time?
Oor Wullie: **Aye, he's a braw watch dog!**

What did Harry say when he sat on sandpaper?
Oor Wullie: **Rough, rough!**

Can Harry sit up and beg?
Oor Wullie: **Oh, aye. Yesterday
he came hame wi' two
pounds twenty pence!**

5

Funny Food

Mince an' tatties are his favourite food,
So Ma dishes them up . . . when he's
been good.

Where were chips first fried?
Oor Wullie: **Greece!**

What's the best thing to put in a pie?
Oor Wullie: **Yer teeth!**

Why did the banana go to the doctor?
Oor Wullie: **Because it wisnae peeling well!**

Why does nobody starve on Auchenshoogle Beach?
Oor Wullie: **It's because of aw
the sand which is there!**

Why did the Scottish potatoes change their nationality?
Oor Wullie: **Because they wanted
to be French fries!**

What do you get if you cross a chicken with a zebra?
Oor Wullie: **A four-legged meal wi' its
ain barcode!**

Why shouldn't you tell secrets on a farm?
Oor Wullie: **Because the potatoes have eyes an' the corn has ears!**

Where do you get chilli beans?
Oor Wullie: **At the North Pole!**

If crocodiles make shoes what do bananas make?
Oor Wullie: **Slippers!**

What happens if you sit on a tube of chocolate sweets?
Oor Wullie: **You become a right smartie-pants!**

Why are school cooks cruel?
Oor Wullie: **Because they batter fish an' beat eggs!**

Why don't you eat up your mince? It's full of iron.
Oor Wullie: **Nae wonder it's so tough!**

How do you make jam roly-poly?
Oor Wullie: **Push the jar off the table!**

What cheese is made backwards?
Oor Wullie: **Edam!**

Why should you never tell an egg a joke?
Oor Wullie: **It might jist crack up!**

What do you call a cashew in a rocket?
Oor Wullie: **An astronut!**

What do mermaids have on their toast?
Oor Wullie: **Mermalade!**

What do you get if you cross gunpowder and an egg?
Oor Wullie: **A boom-meringue!**

*What is made of dough, is a hundred and
fifty feet high, and is in Italy?*
Oor Wullie: **The Leaning Tower o' Pizza!**

How did the baker mop up the spilt milk?
Oor Wullie: **He used sponge cake!**

*What has no beginning, no end, and
has nothing in the middle?*
Oor Wullie: **A doughnut!**

Why did the jelly wobble?
Oor Wullie: **Because it saw the milk shake!**

How do you make an apple puff?
Oor Wullie: **Chase it roond the park!**

Where do they sell thick chips in Scotland?
Oor Wullie: **Dum-Fries!**

*Can I have the fastest
bun in the world?*
Oor Wullie: **Too late,
it's scone!**

6

Really Funny
Riddles

Oor Wullie's aye so full o' fizz,
An' he's awfy good at any quiz.

Why are Grandma's teeth like stars?
Oor Wullie: **Because they come oot at night!**

What did your bucket say tae the wee bucket?
Oor Wullie: **Yer looking a little pail!**

What happens when a clock is still hungry?
Oor Wullie: **It goes back four seconds!**

What has one head, one foot and four legs?
Oor Wullie: **A bed!**

What gets bigger the more you take away?
Oor Wullie: **A hole!**

What is brown, has a tail, a head but no legs?
Oor Wullie: **A penny!**

What do angels say when they answer the phone?
Oor Wullie: **Halo!**

*Wee Eck's Pa has three sons: Calum,
Stuart and who else?*
Oor Wullie: **Wee Eck!**

*What did Batman and Robin become when
they were run over by a bus?*
Oor Wullie: **Flatman and Ribbon!**

Why did the computer require glasses?
Oor Wullie: **To improve its web-sight!**

What do you get if you swing from trees in the park?
Oor Wullie: **Sore hands an' sore arms!**

Why is perfume obedient?
Oor Wullie: **Because it goes where it's scent!**

*What happened to
your wooden cartie with
wooden wheels and
wooden engine?*
Oor Wullie:
It wooden go!

Why did the crab blush?
Oor Wullie: **Because the sea weed!**

What do mummy brushes say to baby brushes every night?
Oor Wullie: **Go tae sweep!**

What goes up but never comes down?
Oor Wullie: **Yer age!**

What happens if you fly from Majorca to Edinburgh?
Oor Wullie: **You get awfa sore arms!**

What do criminals and pub landlords have in common?
Oor Wullie: **They both spend a lot o' time behind bars!**

What goes ha ha ha, plop!
Oor Wullie: **Someone laughing their heid aff!**

What happened to the athlete whose trainers were too small?
Oor Wullie: **He suffered the agony of defeat!**

What starts with a 'P' and ends with an 'E', and has millions of letters in it?
Oor Wullie: **Post Office!**

When does the cart come before the horse?
Oor Wullie: **In the dictionary!**

What immediately breaks when you speak?
Oor Wullie: **Silence!**

What did the Scottish fisherman who lived on an island say?
Oor Wullie: **Iona boat!**

What is a cartoon?
Oor Wullie: **A song you sing in an automobile!**

Why did the balloon burst?
Oor Wullie: **Because it saw the lolly pop!**

How do trains hear?
Oor Wullie: **Through their engine-eers!**

Who can jump higher than a house?
Oor Wullie: **Anyone. A house cannae jump!**

What is full of holes but still holds water?
Oor Wullie: **A sponge!**

What did the caveman give his girlfriend on Valentine's Day?
Oor Wullie: **Ugs and kisses!**

What has two hands, a face, always runs, but never moves?
Oor Wullie: **A clock!**

How do fleas travel around?
Oor Wullie: **By itch hiking!**

What happened to the inflatable boy?
Oor Wullie: **He let himself doon!**

What stays in a corner, but travels the world?
Oor Wullie: **A stamp!**

*What happened to the refuse collector
who complained he didn't have anywhere
to put the rubbish?*
Oor Wullie: **He got the sack!**

What did the paper clip say to the magnet?
Oor Wullie: **Yer so attractive. Ah feel myself
drawn tae you!**

*What happens if you eat
shoe polish and yeast?*
Oor Wullie: **Every morning
you'll rise an' shine!**

53

What gets wetter the more it dries?
Oor Wullie: **A towel!**

What did one pencil say to the other?
Oor Wullie: **Ah must say yer looking sharp!**

What do you get if you cross a fish with an elephant?
Oor Wullie: **Swimming trunks!**

Where do bees do the bathroom?
Oor Wullie: **At the BP service station!**

What do you call a baby monkey?
Oor Wullie: **A chimp aff the old block!**

What do you call a belt with a clock on it?
Oor Wullie: **A waist o' time!**

Why do some fish live in salt water?
Oor Wullie: **Because pepper makes them sneeze!**

What do you get if you lose weight?
Oor Wullie: **The Nobelly Prize!**

*What do you get if you pull your
knickers up to your armpits?*
Oor Wullie: **A chest o' drawers!**

How does Jack Frost get to work?
Oor Wullie: **By Icicle!**

What should you do if you swallow a light bulb?
Oor Wullie: **Spit it oot an'
you'll be delighted!**

*What season of the year is it when
you're on a trampoline?*
Oor Wullie: **Spring time!**

*What is the best day
to go to the beach?*
Oor Wullie: **On a
sun-day!**

What goes through towns, over hills and rivers, but never moves?
Oor Wullie: **Roads!**

What did the one lift say to the other lift?
Oor Wullie: **Ah think ah'm comin' doon wi' somethin'!**

Why did the traffic light turn red?
Oor Wullie: **Well, you would too if you had tae change in the street!**

What has four wheels and flies?
Oor Wullie: **The scaffie's lorry!**

Why is it unsafe to doze off on trains?
Oor Wullie: **Because they run over sleepers!**

Why did the bank robber take a bath?
Oor Wullie: **Because he wanted tae make a clean getaway!**

Why couldn't the pirate play at cards?
Oor Wullie: **He wis sitting on the deck!**

*What do poor people have, rich people don't have,
and if you eat it you die?*
Oor Wullie: **Nothing!**

What do you call a Scotsman wearing a coat?
Oor Wullie: **Mac!**

What month do soldiers dislike?
Oor Wullie: **March!**

What did the blanket say to the bed?
Oor Wullie: **Dinnae worry, ah've
got you covered!**

*What happened when the cat
swallowed a ball of wool?*
Oor Wullie: **It had mittens!**

Why did the tug-of-war team lose the match?
Oor Wullie: **They pushed!**

Which is the fastest: cold or hot?
Oor Wullie: **Hot, because you can always catch a cold!**

What did the station porter wear on her feet?
Oor Wullie: **Platform shoes!**

Why did the man with one hand cross the street?
Oor Wullie: **To get to the second hand shop!**

What did the one snowman say to the other snowman?
Oor Wullie: **That's funny, ah can smell carrots, too!**

Why did Fat Bob throw a clock out of his window?
Oor Wullie: **Because he wanted tae see time fly!**

*What did the Australian try to do when he received
a new boomerang for his birthday?*
Oor Wullie: **Throw away his auld one!**

What goes up when the rain comes down?
Oor Wullie: **A brolly!**

What did the girl light bulb say to the boy light bulb?
Oor Wullie: **Ah love you watts and watts!**

What kind of lights did Noah have on the Ark?
Oor Wullie: **Flood lights!**

What do you do after shaking hands with a monster?
Oor Wullie: **Count yer fingers!**

*What's the difference between a
bus driver and a cold in the head?*
Oor Wullie: **A bus driver
knows the stops, an' a cold
in the heid stops the nose.**

What's the quietest game in the world?
Oor Wullie: **Tenpin bowling, because you can hear a pin drop!**

Why was the man fired at the orange juice factory?
Oor Wullie: **Because he couldnae concentrate!**

What do you call a country where everyone drives red cars?
Oor Wullie: **A red carnation!**

What did the alien say to the gardener?
Oor Wullie: **Take me tae your weeder!**

What did one invisible man say to the other invisible man?
Oor Wullie: **It's nice no' to see you again!**

Why do fairy godmothers make such good football coaches?
Oor Wullie: **Because they help you tae get tae the ball!**

Why did the computer keep sneezing?
Oor Wullie: **Because it had a virus!**

What's the best thing to do if a monster breaks down your front door?
Oor Wullie: **Run oot the back door!**

What does a goalkeeper do in his leisure time?
Oor Wullie: **He surfs the net!**

What does 'www' stand for?
Oor Wullie: **Wee Willie Winkie!**

What do corduroy pillows make?
Oor Wullie: **Headlines!**

Why do golfers have two pairs of trousers?
Oor Wullie: **In case they get a hole in one!**

61

Why are robots never afraid?
Oor Wullie: **Because they hae nerves o' steel!**

What did the cowboy say to the German garage?
Oor Wullie: **Audi, partner!**

Where do swimmers eat?
Oor Wullie: **At the pool table!**

If you have an oil lamp, a fireplace and a stove, what do you light first?
Oor Wullie: **A match!**

What runs but can't walk?
Oor Wullie: **Water!**

What's an astronaut's favourite place on a computer?
Oor Wullie: **The Space Bar!**

What did the occupants of the tree say to the wind?
Oor Wullie: **Please leaf us alone!**

Which sport are waitresses good at?
Oor Wullie: **Tennis, because most serve well!**

Why does moon rock taste better than earth rock?
Oor Wullie: **Because it's a little meteor!**

What can go up a chimney down,
but can't go up a chimney up?
Oor Wullie: **A brolly!**

Why was the brush late?
Oor Wullie: **It over swept!**

What stories do seamen tell their children?
Oor Wullie: **Ferry stories!**

How did the hairdresser
win the race?
Oor Wullie: **He took**
a short cut!

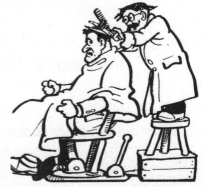

How many times did the boy pass wind?
Oor Wullie: **Quite a phew!**

What did the tie say to the hat?
Oor Wullie: **You go on a head,
ah'll hang around!**

*Why couldn't the Native American Indian
get a room in the hotel?*
Oor Wullie: **He didnae have a reservation!**

What is a lady magician called?
Oor Wullie: **Trixie!**

What has a bottom at the top?
Oor Wullie: **Legs!**

*What happened when the ship carrying
red and black paint sank?*
Oor Wullie: **The crew were marooned
oan a desert island!**

What's the quickest way to make anti-freeze?
Oor Wullie: **Hide her nightie!**

Who designed Noah's ship?
Oor Wullie: **An ark-itect!**

What do you call a man with a stamp on his head?
Oor Wullie: **Frank!**

Why will Cinderella never play football?
Oor Wullie: **Because she keeps running away frae the ball, has the wrong footwear, an' has a pumpkin fur a coach!**

What is an ig?
Oor Wullie: **An Eskimo's house withoot a toilet!**

What happened when the Highland dancer washed his kilt?
Oor Wullie: **He couldnae dae a fling wi' it!**

7

HA-HA-Halloween

If Wullie ventures oot the nicht,
He's goin' tae get an awfu' fricht.

*I have two noses, three eyes
and four ears. What am I?*
Oor Wullie: **Ugly!**

What do you get if you cross a snowman with a vampire?
Oor Wullie: **Frostbite!**

What do you call an unmarried vampire?
Oor Wullie: **A bat-chelor!**

Why are cemeteries very noisy places?
Oor Wullie: **It's because o' all the coughin's!**

What do you get if you cross a werewolf with a flower?
Oor Wullie: **Ah don't know, but ah'm certainly
no' gonnae smell it tae find oot!**

*What did the mummy skeleton say to her
son when he told a lie?*
Oor Wullie: **You cannae fool me. Ah can see
right through you!**

Why didn't the skeleton cross the road?
Oor Wullie: **It didnae have the guts!**

What do you call two witches who share a room?
Oor Wullie: **Broom mates!**

What exam was the student vampire studying for?
Oor Wullie: **His blood test!**

What skeleton was once the Emperor of France?
Oor Wullie: **Napoleon Bone-apart!**

What happens to angry witches when they ride their broomsticks?
Oor Wullie: **They fly off the handle!**

What do you call a skeleton who won't get out of bed in the morning?
Oor Wullie: **Lazy bones!**

Why do witches all wear name badges?
Oor Wullie: **So you ken which witch is witch!**

What kind of a dream are you having if it is all about a man in a tin suit chasing you?
Oor Wullie: **A knightmare!**

What is a ghost's favourite soup?
Oor Wullie: **Scream of tomato!**

What did the mummy ghost say to the baby ghost?
Oor Wullie: **Only spook when yer spooken to!**

Where do baby ghosts go during the day?
Oor Wullie: **Dayscare nurseries!**

What do you call a pixie with a sore leg?
Oor Wullie: **A hoblin goblin!**

Where does Dracula stay in New York?
Oor Wullie: **At the Vampire State Building!**

When do ghosts haunt multi-storey blocks of flats?
Oor Wullie: **When they are in high spirits!**

Why does Dracula have no friends?
Oor Wullie: **Because he's a bit o'
a pain in the neck!**

What do witches put on their sandwiches?
Oor Wullie: **Scream cheese!**

Why wouldn't the skeleton go to school?
Oor Wullie: **Because his heart wisnae in it!**

What do you call a witch's garage?
Oor Wullie: **A broom cupboard!**

*What did the estate agent
say to the ghost?*
Oor Wullie: **Sorry, but we
hae nothing suitable for
haunting at the moment!**

What do dragons wear to school?
Oor Wullie: **Blazers!**

What do you call a witch's motorbike?
Oor Wullie: **A broooom stick!**

What do ghosts eat at lunchtime?
Oor Wullie: **Spookgetti!**

Who sends Dracula letters?
Oor Wullie: **His fang club!**

What do you get if you cross a witch with an ice cube?
Oor Wullie: **A cold spell!**

Which airline do ghosts travel on?
Oor Wullie: **British Scareways!**

What can't you give a headless ghost?
Oor Wullie: **A headache!**

What did the ghost teacher say to her class?
Oor Wullie: **Look at the board an' ah'll go through it again!**

How do you make a witch itch?
Oor Wullie: **Take awa the 'w'!**

What kind of streets do ghosts haunt?
Oor Wullie: **Dead ends!**

What subject in school would be easy for a witch?
Oor Wullie: **Spell-ing!**

What do you get if you cross a ghost with Bambi?
Oor Wullie: **Bamboo!**

What position does a zombie play at fitba?
Oor Wullie: **A ghoulkeeper!**

What do schools do to naughty witches?
Oor Wullie: **They ex-spell them!**

What do witches put on their hair?
Oor Wullie: **Scare spray!**

Why did the cowboy take hay to bed?
Oor Wullie: **He wanted tae feed his nightmare!**

How many vampires can you fit into Hampden Park if it's empty?
Oor Wullie: **One. After that it's no' empty!**

What sort of ship do vampires sail on?
Oor Wullie: **Blood vessels!**

What do you get if you cross a gargoyle and an owl?
Oor Wullie: **An ugly bird that doesnae give a hoot!**

What game do baby ghosts play at parties?
Oor Wullie: **Haunt the thimble!**

What's Dr Jekyll's favourite game?
Oor Wullie: **Hyde an' Seek!**

Where do Native American Indian ghosts sleep?
Oor Wullie: **In creepee teepees!**

Why do witches love computers?
Oor Wullie: **Because they hae spell checkers!**

Why do vampires never get fat?
Oor Wullie: **They eat necks tae nothing!**

Primrose: *I think I'm a witch, Wullie.*
Oor Wullie: **Well, you had better lie down for a spell!**

Why do ghosts make poor magicians?
Oor Wullie: **You can see right through their tricks!**

What goes moorb moorb?
Oor Wullie: **A witch flying backwards on her motorbike!**

What do you get if you cross a ghost with the Loch Ness Monster?
Oor Wullie: **Somethin' that is very seldom seen!**

Why do witches change people into frogs?
Oor Wullie: **Because if they turned them intae lions, they might eat them!**

Why do witches fly on broomsticks?
Oor Wullie: **Because Hoovers are far too heavy!**

What part of a newspaper does a ghost read?
Oor Wullie: **The horror-scope!**

What is black and has eight wheels?
Oor Wullie: **A witch's cat oan roller skates!**

What do you do when 50 zombies surround your house?
Oor Wullie: **Hope it's Halloween!**

What kind of ghosts haunt hospitals?
Oor Wullie: **Surgical spirits!**

What do you call a nervous witch?
Oor Wullie: **A twitch!**

What do you call a fat pumpkin?
Oor Wullie:
A plumpkin!

8

Christmas Crackers

Santa's due doon Wullie's lum,
Wi' plenty presents fur oor chum.

Why does Santa go down chimneys?
Oor Wullie: **Because it soots him!**

What do Santa's elves do after school?
Oor Wullie: **Their gnomework!**

What is Santa's nationality?
Oor Wullie: **North Polish!**

What does Tarzan sing at Christmas?
Oor Wullie: **Jungle Bells!**

Who looks after Santa when he's ill?
Oor Wullie: **The National Elf Service!**

Who is a snowman's favourite aunt?
Oor Wullie: **Aunt Arctica!**

When does Santa say 'oh, oh, oh'?
Oor Wullie: **When he's walking backwards!**

*What's the difference between the English alphabet
and the Christmas alphabet?*
Oor Wullie: **The Christmas alphabet has Noel!**

*What did Santa say when his wife asked
about the water running down the window?*
Oor Wullie: **It's rain dear!**

*If an athlete gets athlete's foot,
what does a spaceman get?*
Oor Wullie: **Missile toe!**

Which of Santa's reindeer has bad manners?
Oor Wullie: **Rude-olph!**

Where is Turkey?
Oor Wullie: **In ma tummy oan Christmas Day!**

*What do snowmen
have for breakfast?*
Oor Wullie:
Frosted Flakes!

*What happened to the man who stole
the Christmas calendar?*
Oor Wullie: **He got twelve months!**

What is the best Christmas present of all?
Oor Wullie: **A broken drum.
You cannae beat it!**

*What's the difference between
Santa's reindeer and a knight?*
Oor Wullie: **One slays the dragon an'
the other's draggin' the sleigh!**

What did Adam say the night before Christmas?
Oor Wullie: **It's Christmas, Eve!**

What is Rudolf's favourite charity day?
Oor Wullie: **Red Nose Day!**

Why does Santa have a garden?
Oor Wullie: **So he can hoe, hoe, hoe!**

What do you get if you cross an iPad
with a Christmas tree?
Oor Wullie: **A pine-apple!**

What do you call someone who is afraid of Santa?
Oor Wullie: **Claus-terphobic!**

What's brown and sneaks quietly round
the Christmas dinner table?
Oor Wullie: **Mince spies!**

What do you get if you cross Santa with a duck?
Oor Wullie: **Christmas quackers!**

What do you call an elf who sings?
Oor Wullie: **A wrapper!**

Where did Santa learn to
slide down a chimney?
Oor Wullie: **At a**
chimn-asium!

9

OoR WULLie
and
Primrose Paterson

Posh Primrose loves oor Sunday Post star,
And he likes her fine . . . but best from afar!

Primrose: *Wullie, what flowers grow much better if you give them a kiss?*
Oor Wullie: **Two-lips!**

Primrose: *Why do I sprinkle sugar on my pillow at night?*
Oor Wullie: **So you can have sweet dreams!**

Oor Wullie: **It must be awfa hard for you tae eat, Primrose.**
Primrose: *Why is that?*
Oor Wullie: **Because you canny bear tae stop talking!**

Primrose: *I didn't come here to be insulted.*
Oor Wullie: **Oh, an' where do you usually go?**

Primrose: *What would you do, Wullie, if another girl rolled her eyes at you?*
Oor Wullie: **Ah'd roll them back!**

Primrose: *Oh, Wullie, what should I wear that will never go out of fashion?*
Oor Wullie: **A smile, Primrose!**

Oor Wullie: **Why are you jumping up and doon, Primrose?**
Primrose: *Well, I've got to take a cough medicine, and it says on the bottle, 'shake well before using'.*

Primrose: *My mother says my legs look like matchsticks.*
Oor Wullie: **Well they dae look like sticks, but they certainly dinnae match!**

Oor Wullie: **Primrose, is that perfume ah smell?**
Primrose: *It is, and yes, you do!*

Primrose: *Wullie, when I grow up I want to be a ballet dancer.*
Oor Wullie: **Well, Primrose, that'll certainly keep you on yer toes!**

10

Auchenshoogle's Countryside

Wullie loves the hills and heather,
In spring, in summer an' cauld weather.

What did Pa bee say when he got home from work?
Oor Wullie: **Honey, ah'm home!**

What happened to the magic tractor?
Oor Wullie: **It went doon the track an' turned intae a field!**

What was the snail doing on Auchenshoogle's main road?
Oor Wullie: **Aboot twa miles a week!**

What do other cows sing when one of them has a birthday?
Oor Wullie: **Happy birthday to moo!**

What do you call a month of rain in Auchenshoogle?
Oor Wullie: **Summer!**

Why do cows moo?
Oor Wullie: **Because their horns dinnae work!**

Why do people ride on horses?
Oor Wullie: **Because they're too heavy tae carry!**

Why didn't the cow worry when she lost her voice?
Oor Wullie: **Because no moos is good moos!**

How do hedgehogs play leapfrog?
Oor Wullie: **Awfa carefully!**

What goes in pink and comes out blue?
Oor Wullie: **Swimmers at Auchenshoogle beach!**

What did the mummy bee say to the baby bee?
Oor Wullie: **Beehive yourself!**

Why do chickens dislike people?
Oor Wullie: **They beat eggs!**

*What do you get if you cross a chicken
with a cement-mixer?*
Oor Wullie: **A brick-layer!**

What's brown and sounds like a bell?
Oor Wullie: **Dung!**

*What do you get when you cross a pig
with a karate champion?*
Oor Wullie: **Pork chops!**

*What do you call a cockerel that wakes
you in the morning?*
Oor Wullie: **An alarm cluck!**

What is cowhide used for?
Oor Wullie: **Holding coos th'gither!**

Why did the one-eyed chicken cross the road?
Oor Wullie: **Tae get tae the Bird's Eye shop!**

Why has a milking stool only got three legs?
Oor Wullie: **Because the coo has the udder!**

What do you call a sleeping bull?
Oor Wullie: **A bulldozer!**

What's a horse's favourite sport?
Oor Wullie: **Stable tennis!**

*What happened to the clever boy
who sat under a cow?*
Oor Wullie: **He got a pat
oan the head!**

What do hedgehogs say when they kiss?
Oor Wullie: **Ouch!**

*Why did you laugh when
the cow fell over?*
Oor Wullie: **There's no
point in crying over
spilled milk!**

Why did the Auchenshoogle farmer plough his field with a steamroller?
Oor Wullie: **Because he wanted mashed potatoes!**

What is a tree's least favourite month?
Oor Wullie: **Sep-TIMBER!**

What's a scarecrow's favourite food?
Oor Wullie: **STRAW-berries!**

Why did the birds move to the country?
Oor Wullie: **The rent was CHEEP!**

What do you get when you cross a hedgehog with a giraffe?
Oor Wullie: **A six-foot toothbrush!**

How do rabbits keep their fur neat?
Oor Wullie: **They use a harebrush!**

How do you stop milk turning sour?
Oor Wullie: **Keep it in the coo!**

How do bulls pay for their shopping?
Oor Wullie: **They 'charge' it to the farmer!**

What do you call a multi-storey pig pen?
Oor Wullie: **A sty-scraper!**

Where do trees store their belongings?
Oor Wullie: **In their trunks!**

What do you call a rabbit with fleas?
Oor Wullie: **Bugs Bunny!**

What is big, green and can't fly?
Oor Wullie: **A field!**

Where do sheep go for a haircut?
Oor Wullie: **Tae the
ba-ba shop!**

11

OoR WuLLie's Music

Most music is tae Oor Wullie's liking,
At hame, at school or even oot hiking.

Why did the girl sit on the ladder?
Oor Wullie: **She wanted tae reach the high notes!**

What type of music are balloons scared of?
Oor Wullie: **Pop music!**

What is the difference between a fish and a piano?
Oor Wullie: **You cannae tuna fish!**

Why are pianos so noble?
Oor Wullie: **Because they are either upright or grand!**

What do you call a cow that plays a musical instrument?
Oor Wullie: **A moo-sician!**

Why is it difficult to unlock a piano?
Oor Wullie: **Because the keys are inside!**

Why did the musician keep his trumpet in the fridge?
Oor Wullie: **He liked to play cool music!**

Why are pirates good singers?
Oor Wullie: **They sail on the high C's!**

Which part of a snake is musical?
Oor Wullie: **The scales**

How do you make a band stand?
Oor Wullie: **Take their chairs away!**

How do you fix a broken tuba?
Oor Wullie: **With a tuba glue!**

When is the water in the shower like the bagpipes?
Oor Wullie: **When it's piping hot!**

99

12

OoR WULLie
and the
WORld o· NaTuRe

The moon and the stars fill him wi' awe,
Though he's doon tae earth wi' his fitba.

What do you call a fish with no eyes?
Oor Wullie: **A Fsh!**

What did the ground say to the earthquake?
Oor Wullie: **You really crack me up!**

When does the moon become heavy?
Oor Wullie: **When it's full!**

What falls but never hits the ground?
Oor Wullie: **The temperature!**

What do you get if you cross a planet with a silver cup?
Oor Wullie: **A constellation prize!**

What did one volcano say to the other volcano?
Oor Wullie: **I lava you!**

What has five eyes that are always wet?
Oor Wullie: **The Mississippi River!**

*What washes up on Auchenshoogle's
smallest beaches?*
Oor Wullie: **Microwaves!**

What did the cloud say to the lightning?
Oor Wullie: **Yer absolutely shocking!**

What do clouds wear?
Oor Wullie: **Thunderwear!**

What is the opposite of a cold front?
Oor Wullie: **A warm back!**

What kind of ticks are found on the moon?
Oor Wullie: **Luna-ticks!**

*How can you tell if the sea
at Auchenshoogle beach
is friendly?*
Oor Wullie: **It gives
me a wave!**

13

OoR WULLie
and
PC Murdoch,
Auchenshoogle's
Long-sufferin' Bobby

P.C. MURDOCH.

THE BIGGEST FEET
IN THE FORCE.
MAKES MAIR NOISE
THAN A PAIR O'HORSE!

Come here, Wullie, frae me you cannae hide,
Whit's yer name, yer age, and
whaur dae you bide?

Oor Wullie: **Whit dae you call a policeman who flies?**
PC Murdoch: *A heli-cop-ter!*

Oor Wullie: **Why did the book join the police force?**
PC Murdoch: *It wanted tae go undercover, Wullie!*

Oor Wullie: **What does a lawyer call his daughter?**
PC Murdoch: *Sue!*

Oor Wullie: **What sort of sentence wid you get if you broke the laws o' gravity?**
PC Murdoch: *A suspended one, Wullie!*

Oor Wullie: **What are two robbers called?**
PC Murdoch: *A pair o' nickers, Wullie!*

Oor Wullie: What did you do with the man who stole the lorry filled with rhubarb?

PC Murdoch: *Ah pit him in custard-y!*

Oor Wullie: Whit happened at the robbery in the Auchenshoogle laundry yesterday?

PC Murdoch: *Four clothes-pegs held up twa shirts, Wullie!*

Oor Wullie: Are pictures allowed in jail?

PC Murdoch: *Only if they're framed, Wullie!*

PC Murdoch: *Halt! Why have you got all that rubbish on yer bike, Wullie?*

Oor Wullie: Ah'm recycling it, PC Murdoch!

Oor Wullie: What dae lawyers wear to court?

PC Murdoch: *Lawsuits!*

14

OoR WULLie's Gang-
Fat Bob, Soapy Soutar
and Wee Eck

Fat Bob, Soapy Soutar, an' Wee Eck are his gang,
Tellin' jokes, bein' noisy, doin' things aw wrang!

Oor Wullie: **Bob, there's a big red thing oan your face.**
Fat Bob: *Whit is it?*
Oor Wullie: **Yer nose!**

Oor Wullie: **Why did you go oot wi' a prune, Fat Bob?**
Fat Bob: *Because ah couldnae get a date!*

Wee Eck: *What kind o' tea dae fitba' players drink?*
Oor Wullie: **Penal tea!**

Oor Wullie: **Hey, Soapy, have you heard aboot the idiot who goes aroon saying 'no'?**
Soapy Soutar: *No.*
Oor Wullie: **Oh, so it's you!**

Fat Bob: *Why do some fitba' players take a bit o' rope on to the pitch with them?*
Oor Wullie: **They're the skippers!**

Oor Wullie: **Bob, do you put oan a pair o' clean socks every day?**

Fat Bob: *Aye, Wullie, but at the end of the week ah cannae get ma feet intae ma boots!*

Fat Bob: *Wee Eck smells like a fish since he fell in the sea at Auchenshoogle beach.*

Oor Wullie: **Poor sole!**

Fat Bob: *Wullie, what did you give Soapy Soutar for his birthday?*

Oor Wullie: **Measles!**

Soapy Soutar: *Why do fitba' players admire magicians?*

Oor Wullie: **Because they dae hat tricks!**

Soapy Soutar: *Why are pirates called pirates?*

Oor Wullie: **Because they arrrrr!**

Fat Bob: *What do you think the librarian at the Auchenshoogle library would say if Andy Murray walked in an' asked for books on tennis aces?*

Oor Wullie: **Now, mak sure you return them, Andy!**

Fat Bob: *And what do you think Andy Murray would say if you told him tennis seems an awfy noisy game?*

Oor Wullie: **He'd probably blame the racquet!**

Soapy Soutar: *The ointment the doctor gave me is making ma hands smart.*

Oor Wullie: **There is only one answer tae that. Rub some on yer heid!**

Soapy Soutar: *Wullie, how are you getting on with your trampoline?*

Oor Wullie: **Oh, up and doon, you know!**

Fat Bob: *Can you stand on your heid, Wullie?*

Oor Wullie: **Ah've tried, but I cannae get ma feet up high enough!**

Wee Eck: *What do you call a girl behind a goal?*
Oor Wullie: **Annette!**

Fat Bob: *What runs along the edge of a fitba'*
pitch but never moves?
Oor Wullie: **The sideline!**

Wee Eck: *You're looking as though ye're dizzy, Wullie.*
Oor Wullie: **Aye, ah've been doin' a lot o' good turns today.**

Oor Wullie: **Whit's your Pa getting for Christmas?**
Fat Bob: *Fat and bald!*

Oor Wullie: **Listen, Eck, I bet I can make you speak like a Native American Indian.**
Wee Eck: *How?*
Oor Wullie: **See!**

15

Auchenshoogle's Dentist

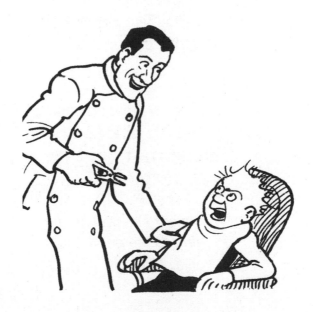

Wullie cleans his teeth wi' care,
Tae keep him awa frae the dentist's chair

What did the judge say to the dentist?
Oor Wullie: **Do you swear to pull the tooth, the whole tooth, an' nothin' but the tooth?**

What did one tooth say to the other?
Oor Wullie: **There's gold in them there fills!**

Why did the Queen go to the dentist?
Oor Wullie: **Tae have her teeth crowned!**

Has your tooth stopped hurting?
Oor Wullie: **Ah dinnae know. The dentist kept it!**

What reward do you get for going to the dentist?
Oor Wullie: **A little plaque!**

What do dentists call their X-rays?
Oor Wullie: **Tooth-pics!**

What did the one tooth say to the other tooth?
Oor Wullie: **Ah've got a date.
The dentist is going tae tak me oot!**

What two letters do teeth dislike?
Oor Wullie: **D K!**

What do you call a Scottish dentist?
Oor Wullie: **Phil McCavity!**

Who has the most dangerous job in Transylvania?
Oor Wullie: **Dracula's Dentist!**

*When is the best time
to go to the dentist?*
Oor Wullie: **Tooth-hurty!**

16

Auchenshoogle's Doctor

When Wullie's feelin' low and ill,
Ma taks him there tae get a pill.

What did the doctor say to the man who thought he was a chocolate biscuit?
Oor Wullie: **He said, 'Yer no' a chocolate biscuit. Yer crackers!'**

When do doctors become angry?
Oor Wullie: **When they run oot o' patients!**

Why did the pillow go to the doctor?
Oor Wullie: **It was feelin' aw stuffed up!**

Where do sick ships go?
Oor Wullie: **Tae the doc-k!**

What would the doctor say to you if you thought you were a spoon?
Oor Wullie: **Dinnae stir!**

What did the doctor say to the man who snored so loudly he woke himself up?
Oor Wullie: **Go an' sleep in another room!**

*What did the doctor say to the boy who
thought he was budgie?*
Oor Wullie: **Ye'll need tae go tae a vet.
Ah cannae tweet ye!**

Oor Wullie: **Help, doctor, I've swallowed
my pen. What should I do?**
Doctor: *Use a pencil!*

Oor Wullie: **Whit is a dimple, doctor?**
Doctor: *A pimple going the wrong way.*

*What did the doctor say to the man
who had difficulty breathing?*
Oor Wullie: **Dinnae worry, ah'll give you
somethin' that will pit a stop tae that!**

*Why did the bird go
to the doctor?*
Oor Wullie:
For tweetment!

Have you ever had trouble with appendicitis?
Oor Wullie: **Only when ah try tae spell it, doctor!**

How do you get rid of a headache?
Oor Wullie: **If you break a window the pane will disappear!**

What did the doctor say to the man who complained he had flat feet?
Oor Wullie: **Have you tried a bicycle pump?**

What did the doctor give you for the raspberry growing out of your ear?
Oor Wullie: **Some cream tae put on it!**

What did the doctor say to you about that insect bite?
Oor Wullie: **He said there wis a nasty bug goin' around!**

How do you stop a head cold getting into your chest?
Oor Wullie: **Tie a knot in yer neck!**

Why do you tiptoe past the medicine cabinet?
Oor Wullie: **Ah didnae want tae wake Ma's sleeping tablets!**

What did the doctor say to the man who complained he was getting smaller?
Oor Wullie: **He said he would just hae tae be a little patient!**

Doctor: *Sorry you were bitten by a wasp. I'll put some cream on it.*
Oor Wullie: **But it will be miles away by noo, doctor!**

What did the doctor say to the man who said his arm became sore when he lifted it up?
Oor Wullie: **Dinnae lift it up!**

What did the doctor say to the man who complained his nose was always running?
Oor Wullie: **Stick oot yer foot an' trip it up!**

Oor Wullie: **Will these blue pills you've given me make me better, doctor?**

Doctor: *Well, none of the other patients I've given them to has ever come back to complain!*

What did the doctor say to the man who thought he was a caterpillar?
Oor Wullie: **Dinnae worry, ye'll soon change!**

What did the doctor say to the man who said he felt like a chocolate sweet?
Oor Wullie: **So dae ah. Have you got any on you?**

What did the doctor say to the boy who complained he had a sore leg?
Oor Wullie: **Try limpin'!**

What did the doctor say to the boy who thought his left side was missing?
Oor Wullie: **Well, at least yer all right noo!**

124

What did the doctor say when the boy asked if the ointment would clear up his spots?
Oor Wullie: **Ah never mak' rash promises!**

What did the doctor say to the man who said he felt like an elastic band?
Oor Wullie: **That's stretching things a bit far!**

What did the doctor say to the boy who said he felt like a greyhound?
Oor Wullie: **Take one o' these pills every two laps!**

What did the doctor say to the boy who said he was boiling?
Oor Wullie: **Simmer doon, son!**

What did the doctor give the lad with wind?
Oor Wullie: **A kite!**

*What did the doctor say to the man who
thought he was invisible?*

Oor Wullie: **Aye, ah can see yer no' all there!**

*What did the doctor say to the man who complained he
got a terrible pain in his eye when he drank tea?*

Oor Wullie: **Try takin' the spoon
oot o' the cup!**

*What did the doctor say when the
patient told him he was a spider?*

Oor Wullie: **Sounds like a web
of lies tae me!**

*What did the doctor say to the man who
thought he was a £500 note?*

Oor Wullie: **Ah suggest you go on holiday.
The change will dae you good!**

*What did the doctor say to the man who
told him he felt like an electric plug?*

Oor Wullie: **That's shocking!**

*What did the doctor say to the man who
complained he had swallowed a grape seed?*
Oor Wullie: **Dinnae worry. You'll be vine soon!**

*What did the doctor say to the boy
who thought he was a bell?*
Oor Wullie: **Take these pills: if they
dinnae work, just ring!**

*What did the doctor say to the boy who thought he
was a pair of curtains?*
Oor Wullie: **Fur goodness' sake, pull
yersel' thegither!**

*What does a doctor give a patient
with a splitting headache?*
Oor Wullie: **Glue!**

*What did the doctor say to
the boy who thought he
was a shepherd?*
Oor Wullie: **Ah widnae lose
any sheep o'er that!**

17

Even More Really Funny Riddles

Oor Wullie sits on his bucket an' thinks
Life is good fun when yer up tae high jinks!

What has twenty-two legs, eleven heads, two wings and goes 'crunch'?
Oor Wullie: **The Auchenshoogle football team when they are aw eating crisps!**

Why did the baker get an electric shock?
Oor Wullie: **He stood on a bun an' a current ran up his leg!**

Why did the biscuit cry?
Oor Wullie: **Because his Ma had been a wafer so long!**

What do old batteries cost?
Oor Wullie: **Nothing. They're free o' charge!**

Why was the sword swallower sent to jail?
Oor Wullie: **Because he coughed an' killed three people!**

Why was the man fired from the calendar factory?
Oor Wullie: **He took a few days off!**

What do you call a fairy that never washes?
Oor Wullie: **Stinkerbell!**

*What have twelve legs, six eyes,
three tails and can't see?*
Oor Wullie: **Three blind mice!**

What do you call a judge with no thumbs?
Oor Wullie: **Just'is fingers!**

*What do you call a man with sports
equipment on his head?*
Oor Wullie: **Jim!**

*Why is it difficult to keep
secrets in winter?*
Oor Wullie: **Because yer
teeth chatter!**

*What happened to the two
bedbugs who fell in love?*
Oor Wullie: **They got married
in the spring!**

What colour is a belch?
Oor Wullie: **Burple!**

Why was the computer cold?
Oor Wullie: **It left its Windows open!**

Why did the computer squeak?
Oor Wullie: **Because someone
stepped on its moose!**

What was Humpty Dumpty wearing when he fell?
Oor Wullie: **A shellsuit!**

*What did the lumberjack say to
his wife in early December?*
Oor Wullie: **No' many chopping
days left till Christmas!**

Why did the boy take a pencil to bed with him?
Oor Wullie: **He needed tae draw the curtains!**

What's a giant's favourite tale?
Oor Wullie: **A tall story!**

What do you give an Auchenshoogle man who has everything for his birthday?
Oor Wullie: **A burglar alarm!**

Why didn't the elephant get on the plane?
Oor Wullie: **It wisnae a Jumbo!**

What did the pencil say to the pencil sharpener?
Oor Wullie: **Stop goin' roon in circles an' get tae the point!**

What do you call a man standing on a pile of leaves?
Oor Wullie: **Russell!**

*Have you heard the joke
about the wheely-bin?*
Oor Wullie: **Aye, an' it's
a load o' rubbish!**

What is purple and fixes pipes?
Oor Wullie: **A plum-er!**

*What's the difference between a boring
teacher and a boring book?*
Oor Wullie: **You can shut the book up!**

Which days of the week are the strongest?
Oor Wullie: **Saturday and Sunday.
The rest are 'weak' days!**

*What happens when you drop a blue
stone into the Red Sea?*
Oor Wullie: **It gets wet!**

What goes mooz?
Oor Wullie: **A plane flying backwards!**

What did mummy corn say to baby corn?
Oor Wullie: **Where's pop corn?**

*Why did the silly sailor grab a
bar of soap when his ship sank?*
Oor Wullie: **He planned tae wash
himself ashore!**

What did the maths book say to the psychiatrist?
Oor Wullie: **Ah have a lot o' problems!**

What happens when the Queen burps?
Oor Wullie: **She issues a Royal Pardon!**

Why are babies good at football?
Oor Wullie: **Because they dribble!**

*What do you call an
unemployed clown?*
Oor Wullie:
Naebody's fool!

*You have a referee in football, an umpire in cricket,
so what do you have in bowls?*
Oor Wullie: **A goldfish!**

*Why did the silly driver always drive
his car in reverse gear?*
Oor Wullie: **Because he knew
the town backwards!**

What's an inkling?
Oor Wullie: **A baby pen!**

What's the difference between a nail and a boxer?
Oor Wullie: **One gets knocked in, an'
the other gets knocked oot!**

What's green and round and goes camping?
Oor Wullie: **A boy sprout!**

What happens if you play table tennis with a bad egg?
Oor Wullie: **First of aw it goes ping,
an' then it goes pong!**

What flies aboot moaning?
Oor Wullie: **A grumble bee!**

What did one magician say to the other magician?
Oor Wullie: **Who was that girl ah sawed you wi' last night!**

What's the difference between a railway guard and a teacher?
Oor Wullie: **One minds the train an' the other trains the mind!**

Why was the submarine sailor thrown out of the navy?
Oor Wullie: **Because he wis caught sleeping wi' the windows open!**

What is pink and wrinkly and belongs to Grandma?
Oor Wullie: **Grandpaw!**

What is a macaw?
Oor Wullie: **A Scottish parrot!**

Why did the flea fail its exams?
Oor Wullie: **It wisnae up tae scratch!**

Which hand do you stir your tea with?
Oor Wullie: **Neither o' them. Ah use a spoon!**

What did the spider do on the computer?
Oor Wullie: **It made a website!**

*Why did the stupid racing driver
make twenty-five pit stops?*
Oor Wullie: **He kept asking
fur directions!**

Why don't centipedes play football?
Oor Wullie: **Because by the time they've
got their boots on it's time tae go hame!**

*What happened when the man plugged
his electric blanket into his toaster?*
Oor Wullie: **He popped oot o'
bed in the morning!**

If Mr and Mrs Bigger had a baby, who would be the biggest of all three?
Oor Wullie: **The baby, because it's a little Bigger!**

Why did the actor fall through the floor?
Oor Wullie: **It wis just a stage he was goin' through!**

What's white and goes up?
Oor Wullie: **A daft snowflake!**

What kind of beans do cannibals like best?
Oor Wullie: **Human beans!**

What happened to the tap dancer?
Oor Wullie: **He fell in the sink!**

What's the difference between teachers and chocolate?
Oor Wullie: **Pupils like chocolate!**

What happens if you cross a sculptor and a werewolf?
Oor Wullie: **You get a Hairy Potter!**

On which day do monsters eat people?
Oor Wullie: **Chews-day!**

Why were the nose and the handkerchief always fighting?
Oor Wullie: **Because every time they met they came tae blows!**

What lies at the bottom of the sea and shivers?
Oor Wullie: **A nervous wreck!**

What do you call a boy and girl fishing together?
Oor Wullie: **Rod and Annette!**

What kinds of cans do you find in Mexico?
Oor Wullie: **Mexi-cans!**

Why can't a girl ask her brother for help?
Oor Wullie: **Because he cannae be a brother an' assist her, too!**

Where can you find giant snails?
Oor Wullie: **At the end o' a giant's fingers an' toes!**

What do you call a married woman with a pair of scissors, a knife and a tin opener?
Oor Wullie: **A Swiss Army Wife!**

What can you put in a box to make it lighter?
Oor Wullie: **Holes!**

What do you call a spaceship that's hot inside?
Oor Wullie: **A Frying saucer!**

How do you get rid of varnish?
Oor Wullie: **Tak awa the 'R'!**

What did the one eye say to the other eye?
Oor Wullie: **Between you and me, somethin' smells!**

*What kind of bed does a
mermaid sleep in?*
Oor Wullie: **A waterbed!**

*Why did the sword swallower
swallow a brolly?*
Oor Wullie: **He wanted tae pit
somethin' away fur a rainy day!**

Why are astronauts so successful?
Oor Wullie: **Because they always
go up in the world!**

Why did the boy wear a nappy to his friend's party?
Oor Wullie: **Because he wis a party-pooper!**

Why is it so hot in a football stadium after a match?
Oor Wullie: **Because aw the fans have left!**

What does everyone overlook?
Oor Wullie: **Their nose!**

Why was the Egyptian girl worried?
Oor Wullie: **Because her Daddy wis a mummy!**

Which hand is best to write with?
Oor Wullie: **Neither. It's best tae write wi' a pen!**

Why was the belt arrested?
Oor Wullie: **Because it held up some trousers!**

What do you call a member of the Royal family who draws large fish?
Oor Wullie: **The Prints of Whales!**

What is the full name of Lee, the boy no one talks to?
Oor Wullie: **Lone Lee!**

When is cricket a crime scene?
Oor Wullie: **When there's a hit an' run!**

Have you got to train as a refuse collector?
Oor Wullie: **No, you pick it up as you go along!**

What's a golfer's favourite letter?
Oor Wullie: **'T'!**

What's the hardest bit about sky-diving?
Oor Wullie: **The ground!**

Why is Britain such a wet country?
Oor Wullie: **Because the Queen has reigned for over sixty years!**

What's the first thing the Queen did when she ascended to the throne?
Oor Wullie: **Sat doon!**

What do you call a deaf monster?
Oor Wullie: **Anything you like!**

What do you get in December that you don't get in any other month?

Oor Wullie: **The letter 'D'!**

What do astronauts eat?

Oor Wullie: **Whatever is in their launch box!**

Why did the two 4's not have a meal?

Oor Wullie: **They already 8!**

Why did the cannibal live on his own?

Oor Wullie: **He was fed up wi' other people!**

Why can't a man living in Auchenshoogle be buried in Dundee?

Oor Wullie: **Because he's still alive!**

What's the laziest part of a car?

Oor Wullie: **The wheels. They're always tyred!**

*What do you call a Roman
Emperor with a cold?*
Oor Wullie: **Julius Sneezer!**

What do you call people with poor eyesight?
Oor Wullie: **Referees!**

What do you call pubs on Mars?
Oor Wullie: **Mars bars!**

Which painting is always complaining?
Oor Wullie: **The Moaning Lisa!**

Why is everyone so tired on 1st April?
Oor Wullie: **Because they've jist finished
a March o' 31 days!**

What is the purpose of an alarm clock?
Oor Wullie: **To wake folks up
who have nae children!**

What do you call a snowman in the summer?
Oor Wullie: **A puddle!**

What has lots of faces, hands, feet and sings?
Oor Wullie: **A choir!**

What is an archaeologist?
Oor Wullie: **Someone whose career is in ruins!**

Where did the general keep his armies?
Oor Wullie: **Up his sleevies!**

How do you make a band stand?
Oor Wullie: **Tak awa' their chairs!**

Who goes puttputtputtputtputtputt?
Oor Wullie: **A very poor golfer!**

18

Chap Door
Fun

There's loads o' knockin' at his door,
So Wullie asks tae find oot more.

Knock, knock.
Oor Wullie: **Wha's there?**
Doughnut.
Oor Wullie: **Doughnut who?**
Doughnut answer the door to strangers!

Knock, knock.
Oor Wullie: **Wha's there?**
Gladys.
Oor Wullie: **Gladys who?**
Gladys you behind the door, Wullie!

Knock, knock.
Oor Wullie: **Wha's there?**
Joe.
Oor Wullie: **Joe who?**
I'm just Joe King!

Knock, knock.
Oor Wullie: **Wha's there?**
Cash.
Oor Wullie: **Cash who?**
No, I'd prefer peanuts!

Knock, knock.
Oor Wullie: **Wha's there?**
Olive.
Oor Wullie: **Olive who?**
Olive just across the road!

Knock, knock.
Oor Wullie: **Wha's there?**
Turnip.
Oor Wullie: **Turnip who?**
Turnip the heating, it's freezing out here!

Knock, knock.
Oor Wullie: **Wha's there?**
Cows.
Oor Wullie: **Cows who?**
No they don't. Cows moo!

Knock, knock.
Oor Wullie: **Wha's there?**
Boo.
Oor Wullie: **Boo who?**
Boo hoo, I've lost my keys!

Knock, knock.
Oor Wullie: **Wha's there?**
Al.
Oor Wullie: **Al who?**
Al let you kiss me if you open the door!

Knock, knock.
Oor Wullie: **Wha's there?**
Eddie.
Oor Wullie: **Eddie who?**
Eddie body home?

Knock, knock.
Oor Wullie: **Wha's there?**
Freeze.
Oor Wullie: **Freeze who?**
Freeze a jolly good fellow!

Knock, knock.
Oor Wullie: **Wha's there?**
Shelby.
Oor Wullie: **Shelby who?**
Shelby coming round the mountain when she comes!

Knock, knock.
Oor Wullie: **Wha's there?**
Bin.
Oor Wullie: **Bin who?**
Bin anywhere nice lately?

Knock, knock.
Oor Wullie: **Wha's there?**
Leaf.
Oor Wullie: **Leaf who?**
Leaf me alone!

Knock, knock.
Oor Wullie: **Wha's there?**
Lettuce.
Oor Wullie: **Lettuce who?**
Lettuce in, Wullie, and you'll find out!

Knock, knock.
Oor Wullie: **Wha's there?**
Justin.
Oor Wullie: **Justin who?**
Just in time for a cup of tea!

Knock, knock.
Oor Wullie: **Wha's there?**
Athena.
Oor Wullie: **Athena who?**
Athena a great film rethently.

Knock, knock.
Oor Wullie: **Wha's there?**
Attish.
Oor Wullie: **Attish who?**
Bless you!

Knock, knock.
Oor Wullie: **Wha's there?**
Arthur.
Oor Wullie: **Arthur who?**
Arthur any sweeties left?

Knock, knock.
Oor Wullie: **Wha's there?**
Norma Lee.
Oor Wullie: **Norma Lee who?**
Norma Lee I'd open the door but I've forgotten my key!

Knock, knock.
Oor Wullie: **Wha's there?**
Tank.
Oor Wullie: **Tank who?**
You're welcome.

Knock, knock.
Oor Wullie: **Wha's there?**
Butter.
Oor Wullie: **Butter who?**
Butter hurry up and open the door I need the loo!

Knock, knock.
Oor Wullie: **Wha's there?**
Figs.
Oor Wullie: **Figs, who?**
Figs the doorbell. It's broken.

Knock, knock.
Oor Wullie: **Wha's there?**
Dishes.
Oor Wullie: **Dishes who?**
*Dishes PC Murdoch.
I want a word wi' you!*

Knock, knock.
Oor Wullie: **Wha's there?**
Annie.
Oor Wullie: **Annie who?**
Annie thing you can do, I can do better!

Knock, knock.
Oor Wullie: **Wha's there?**
Francis.
Oor Wullie: **Francis who?**
Francis a country in Europe!

Knock, knock.
Oor Wullie: **Wha's there?**
Ida.
Oor Wullie: **Ida who?**
Ida terrible day at school today!

Knock, knock.
Oor Wullie: **Wha's there?**
Ice cream soda.
Oor Wullie: **Ice cream soda who?**
Ice cream soda people can hear me!

Knock, knock.
Oor Wullie: **Wha's there?**
Thumping.
Oor Wullie: **Thumping who?**
Thumping green and slimy just went up your leg!

Knock, knock.
Oor Wullie: **Wha's there?**
Police.
Oor Wullie: **Police who?**
Police let me in. It's freezing out here.

Knock, knock.
Oor Wullie: **Wha's there?**
Bell.
Oor Wullie: **Bell who?**
Bell's not working, that's why I knocked.

Knock, knock.
Oor Wullie: **Wha's there?**
Juicy.
Oor Wullie: **Juicy who?**
Juicy my lovely new dress?

19

Funny Fruit
and
Very Funny Veg

Vegetable and fruit come in every shape,
Be they apple, pear, banana or grape.

What happened in the race between the lettuce and the tomato?

Oor Wullie: **The lettuce wis winning but the tomato wis trying tae ketchup!**

What did the bacon say to the tomato?

Oor Wullie: **Lettuce get th'gither!**

Why did the tomato turn red?

Oor Wullie: **It saw the salad dressing!**

Why did the orange stop rolling down the hill?

Oor Wullie: **It ran oot o' juice!**

If you cut two apples into ten pieces, and two pears into ten pieces, what do you get?

Oor Wullie: **A fruit salad!**

What's orange and sounds like a parrot?

Oor Wullie: **A carrot!**

What did the grape say when it got stepped on?
Oor Wullie: **Nothing! It just gave a little wine!**

Why did the baby strawberry cry?
Oor Wullie: **Because his parents were in a jam!**

What do you call two rows of vegetables?
Oor Wullie: **A dual cabbageway!**

What's the difference between a ripe banana and a rotten banana?
Oor Wullie: **Six days!**

What is small and round and giggles a lot?
Oor Wullie: **A wee tickled onion!**

What's worse than finding a worm in your apple?
Oor Wullie: **Finding half a worm!**

MUNCH!

20

Animals, Birds and Insects Are Funny Too!

Lions and tigers he loves them all,
Animals who walk and those who crawl.

Have you ever seen a man-eating tiger?
Oor Wullie: **No, but ah once saw a man eating stovies!**

What's a polygon?
Oor Wullie: **A dead parrot!**

Whit time is it if an elephant sits on your garden fence?
Oor Wullie: **Time tae get a new fence!**

What steps do you take if a lion is chasing you?
Oor Wullie: **Big ones!**

Why can't leopards hide?
Oor Wullie: **Because they're always spotted!**

Why do bees have sticky hair?
Oor Wullie: **Because they use honeycombs!**

Why do cows go to the cinema?
Oor Wullie: **Because they like the mooovies!**

Why did the elephant eat the light bulb?
Oor Wullie: **It wanted a light snack!**

Why did the hen cross the road?
Oor Wullie: **To prove she wisnae chicken!**

What do you call six elephants on a bicycle?
Oor Wullie: **Optimistic!**

What do you get when you cross a cat with a lemon?
Oor Wullie: **A sour puss!**

What is small, red and whispers?
Oor Wullie: **Hoarse raddish!**

What do you get if you cross a dog with a lion?
Oor Wullie: **A very nervous postman!**

Why do polar bears have fur coats?
Oor Wullie: **Well, they'd look awfy silly in blazers!**

Why do giraffes have very long necks?
Oor Wullie: **Because they've very smelly feet!**

How do you know that carrots are good for eyesight?
Oor Wullie: **Well, ah've never seen a rabbit wearin' glasses!**

Have you ever seen a six-foot snake?
Oor Wullie: **Dinnae be daft. Snakes dinnae hae feet!**

What's black and white and eats like a horse?
Oor Wullie: **A zebra!**

How many skunks does it take to make a big stink?
Oor Wullie: **Only a phew!**

How does a monkey get downstairs?
Oor Wullie: **He slides doon on the banana-ster!**

Where do apes buy their clothes?
Oor Wullie: **At jungle sales!**

What do you get if you cross an elephant with a kangaroo?
Oor Wullie: **Holes all o'er Australia!**

What do you say if your see a one-eyed dinosaur?
Oor Wullie: **Do-you-think-he-saw-us?**

In what direction does a chicken run?
Oor Wullie: **Cluck-wise!**

How do you stop elephants charging?
Oor Wullie: **Tak away their credit cards!**

Why didn't the lobster share his sweets?
Oor Wullie: **Because he was shellfish!**

What is a snail?
Oor Wullie: **A slug wearing a crash helmet!**

What do you call an ape who works in a call centre?
Oor Wullie: **A who-rang-atang!**

What do you call a camel wi' three humps?
Oor Wullie: **Humpthree!**

How do you make a goldfish age?
Oor Wullie: **Take away his 'g'!**

How do bees get to school?
Oor Wullie: **They go oan the school buzz!**

What does a baby ape sleep in?
Oor Wullie: **An ape-ri-cot!**

Why did the spider buy a car?
Oor Wullie: **So he could take it oot For a spin!**

What happens if hens drink hot water?
Oor Wullie: **They lay hard-boiled eggs!**

What goes ninety-nine bong, ninety-nine bong?
Oor Wullie: **A centipede wi' a wooden leg!**

Why does a stork stand on one leg?
Oor Wullie: **Because it would Fall o'er if it lifted the other one!**

What did the bird get when it got sick?
Oor Wullie: **Tweet-ment!**

How do dinosaurs pass exams?
Oor Wullie: **With extinction!**

SKELETON of DINOSAUR

What is a bee's favoutite food?
Oor Wullie: **A hum-burger!**

What is the best thing to give a seasick elephant?
Oor Wullie: **Plenty o' room!**

What's black and white and makes a lot of noise?
Oor Wullie: **A zebra wi' a set o' drums!**

How does an idiot call for his dog?
Oor Wullie: **He puts two fingers in his mooth then shouts 'Rover'!**

Whit kind of an ant is good at adding?
Oor Wullie: **An account-ant!**

What do you get if you cross a cow with a mule?
Oor Wullie: **Milk wi' a kick in it!**

What do you get if you cross a kangaroo with a sheep?
Oor Wullie: **A woolly jumper!**

Why did the lion eat the tightrope walker?
Oor Wullie: **He wanted a well-balanced meal!**

On which side does a bird have feathers?
Oor Wullie: **On the outside!**

Which lions live in Auchenshoogle Park?
Oor Wullie: **Dande-lions!**

How do you produce eggs without hens?
Oor Wullie: **Keep ducks!**

Why are budgies always clever?
Oor Wullie: **Because they suck seed!**

How do you communicate with a fish?
Oor Wullie: **Drop him a line!**

Why didn't the butterfly go to the dance?
Oor Wullie: **Because it wis a moth ball!**

Why did the bird fly into the library?
Oor Wullie: **He wis lookin' fur bookworms!**

How do you make an elephant sandwich?
Oor Wullie: **Well, first of aw get a very large loaf o' bread!**

What do you get if you cross an elephant with a flea?
Oor Wullie: **Lots of worried-looking dogs!**

When does 'B' come after 'U'?
Oor Wullie: **When you disturb its hive!**

How do you know when there is an elephant hiding under your bed?
Oor Wullie: **When yer nose hits the ceiling!**

What bird is always out of breath?
Oor Wullie: **A puffin!**

What do you get if you cross a hen with a guitar?
Oor Wullie: **A hen that plays when you pluck it!**

What do you get if you cross an
insect with reindeer horns?
Oor Wullie: **Antlers!**

What's the difference between a tiger and a postbox?
Oor Wullie: **Well, ah'm certainly no' goin' to**
ask you tae post a letter!

What do you call a woodpecker with no beak?
Oor Wullie: **A headbanger!**

What do you get if you pour
hot water down a rabbit hole?
Oor Wullie: **Hot cross**
bunnies!

What do you do with a blue whale?
Oor Wullie: **Cheer it up!**

Why do leopards never take a bath?
Oor Wullie: **They dinnae want to get spotlessly clean!**

How do you count a herd of cows?
Oor Wullie: **With a cowculator!**

What's the best way to speak to the Loch Ness Monster?
Oor Wullie: **From a distance!**

How do you catch a squirrel?
Oor Wullie: **You must climb a tree an' act like a nut!**

Did you know it takes three sheep to make a pullover?
Oor Wullie: **Ah didnae even ken sheep could knit!**

*Whit dae ye get if you cross a
centipede with a parrot?*
Oor Wullie: **A walkie-talkie!**

What animal is out of bounds?
Oor Wullie: **An exhausted kangaroo!**

Where do you take injured wasps?
Oor Wullie: **The waspital!**

*What are prehistoric monsters called when
they are asleep?*
Oor Wullie: **Dino-snores!**

Why did the hedgehog cross the road?
Oor Wullie: **To see his flat mate!**

*What do cats eat for
breakfast?*
Oor Wullie: **Mice
Crispies!**

*What do you get if you cross a
skunk with a boomerang?*
Oor Wullie: **A smell you
cannae get rid o'!**

What did the sick chicken say?
Oor Wullie: **Ah have people pox!**

Where do bees come from?
Oor Wullie: **Stingapore!**

What did the horse say when it fell down?
Oor Wullie: **Ah cannae giddyup!**

What follows behind the Loch Ness Monster?
Oor Wullie: **A great muckle tail!**

Why can't penguins fly?
Oor Wullie: **They're no' tall
enough to be pilots!**

*What did the mummy kangaroo
say to the daddy kangaroo?*
Oor Wullie: **Ah jist hate it when it's raining
an' the children have tae play inside!**

What do you call a fierce monster with no neck?
Oor Wullie: **The Lost Neck Monster!**

What is the world's most unfortunate monster?
Oor Wullie: **The Luck Less Monster!**

How can budgies afford to talk?
Oor Wullie: **Because talk is cheep!**

*What would you call the Loch Ness
Monster if it ate everyone in Scotland?*
Oor Wullie: **Lonely!**

*What do you call a horse
that lives next door?*
Oor Wullie: **A neigh-bour!**

Why did the chicken sit on the egg?
Oor Wullie: **Because it didnae have a chair!**

What lies on its back a hundred feet in the air?
Oor Wullie: **A centipede!**

What do you sing to you budgie on its birthday?
Oor Wullie: **Happy birdy to you!**

How did the chewing gum cross the road?
Oor Wullie: **It wis stuck tae the chicken's foot!**

What do you call a pigeon that skis?
Oor Wullie: **A skean dhu!**

What did the lamb say to its mummy?
Oor Wullie: **I love ewe!**

How do you start a teddy bear race?
Oor Wullie: **You say, 'Ready, teddy, go!'**

What do you get if you cross an ape
with a takeaway restaurant?
Oor Wullie: **Fish an' chimps!**

Are you allowed to feed the lions in Edinburgh Zoo?
Oor Wullie: **No, jist gie them money.**
The notice says: 'Do not Feed. £100 Fine'!

Where do cows go for their holiday in America?
Oor Wullie: **Moo York!**

Why are crabs sent to jail?
Oor Wullie: **They keep pinching things!**

Why did the monkeys leave the circus?
Oor Wullie: **They were Fed up**
workin' For peanuts!

What does one bee say to
another bee on a hot day?
Oor Wullie: **Swarm**
today!

What kind of cats love water?
Oor Wullie: **Octopusses!**

What do tigers say before they hunt?
Oor Wullie: **Let us prey!**

Why was mummy glow-worm unhappy?
Oor Wullie: **Because her children were no' too bright!**

How can you tell you've had an elephant in the fridge?
Oor Wullie: **It leaves footprints in the butter!**

What name did the stupid zookeeper call the zebra?
Oor Wullie: **Spot!**

Who stole the soap in the bath?
Oor Wullie: **The robber duck!**

What happened to the nearsighted porcupine?
Oor Wullie: **He fell in love wi' a pincushion!**

*What do you call a bumble
bee that rings doorbells?*
Oor Wullie: **A humdinger!**

What's the best way to keep fish from smelling?
Oor Wullie: **Cut aff their noses!**

Why is a teddy bear never hungry?
Oor Wullie: **Because he's stuffed!**

How do you catch a rabbit?
Oor Wullie: **Hide behind a tree
and make carrot noises!**

*What did the daddy buffalo say to his
wee boy before he went off on a trip?*
Oor Wullie: **Bi-son!**

*What do you call a
cow eating grass?*
Oor Wullie: **A lawn
mooer!**

Can an ape fly?
Oor Wullie: **Aye, in a hot air-baboon!**

Who's the smelliest ape in the world?
Oor Wullie: **King Pong!**

What do pigs put on when they get sunburnt?
Oor Wullie: **Oinkment!**

What do you call a hungry horse in four letters?
Oor Wullie: **M.T.G.G.!**

What do you get if you cross a carrier pigeon with a woodpecker?
Oor Wullie: **A bird that can carry a message an' is able tae knock on yer door when it arrives!**

Why did the sheep say 'moo'?
Oor Wullie: **It wis learning a foreign language!**

What disguise is worn by an elk?
Oor Wullie: **A False moosetache!**

Why is an elephant big, grey and wrinkled?
Oor Wullie: **Because if he wis small, white an' round he'd be an aspirin!**

What do you get if you cross a homing pigeon with a parrot?
Oor Wullie: **A bird that can ask the way if it gets lost!**

Why won't elephants use their computers?
Oor Wullie: **Because they're afraid o' the mouse!**

What is a caterpillar?
Oor Wullie: **A worm wearing a fur coat!**

*What kind of snake is on a
car windscreen?*
Oor Wullie: **A viper!**

Why did the rabbit cross the road?
Oor Wullie: **It was the chicken's day off!**

Why did the pony cough?
Oor Wullie: **Because it wis a little hoarse!**

How do chickens dance?
Oor Wullie: **Chick to chick!**

Why should you never play games with skunks?
Oor Wullie: **Because if they catch
you cheatin' they'll kick up a stink!**

*Why did the chicken run
on to the football pitch?*
Oor Wullie: **Because the
referee blew fur a fowl!**

*How many tickles does it take to
make an octopus laugh?*
Oor Wullie: **Ten-tickles!**

What do you get if you cross a cockerel and a duck?
Oor Wullie: **A bird that gets up
at the quack of dawn!**

How do you get five elephants into a matchbox?
Oor Wullie: **Tak oot a' the matches first!**

What pet makes the loudest noise?
Oor Wullie: **A trum-pet!**

What do you call a chicken crossing the road?
Oor Wullie: **Poultry in motion!**

*What happened when
the sheepdog ate too
many jellies?*
Oor Wullie: **It got the
collie-wobbles!**

What is as big as an elephant but weighs nothing?
Oor Wullie: **An elephant's shadow!**

What do sharks eat?
Oor Wullie: **Fish and ships!**

What kind of bird sticks to jumpers?
Oor Wullie: **A vel-crow!**

*Why are some fish only found
at the bottom of the sea?*
Oor Wullie: **Because they've
dropped oot o' a school!**

Why did the bee get married?
Oor Wullie: **Because he found his honey!**

*What do you call someone with an
elephant sitting on them?*
Oor Wullie: **Flattened!**

Did everyone enjoy Moby Dick's birthday party?
Oor Wullie: **Aye, they had a whale o' a time!**

What do you give a nervous elephant?
Oor Wullie: **Trunkquillizers!**

How do sheep keep warm in winter?
Oor Wullie: **They use central bleat-ing!**

How can you tell how old a snake is?
Oor Wullie: **If it has a rattle then it must be a baby!**

What do you call a gorilla with a couple of carrots in his ears?
Oor Wullie: **Onything you like. He cannae hear ye!**

What do you get if you cross a duck with the top of the milk?
Oor Wullie: **Cream quackers!**

What do you call an Egyptian mummy who washes dishes?
Oor Wullie: **Pharoah Liquid!**

Why are bananas never lonely?
Oor Wullie: **They come in bunches!**

What can you serve but never eat?
Oor Wullie: **A tennis ball!**

What do you call a man with a stamp on his head?
Oor Wullie: **Frank!**

What happened when Harry visited a flea circus?
Oor Wullie: **He stole the show!**

What do you call a boomerang that doesn't work?
Oor Wullie: **A stick!**

Cheerio!